MR. RED CARPET
FROM HARLEM TO HOLLYWOOD

Written by Elena Neely

Illustrated by Zuri Book Pros

Mr. Red Carpet, From Harlem to Hollywood

ISBN: 979-8-9870721-7-2

Copyright © 2025 Elena M. Neely

Published by Blessons For Living, LLC

www.blessonsforliving.com

Illustrated by: Zuri Book Pros

To Ettastine Neely,
Mother of Tony Neely.
She lived to be 102.

To Tony Neely's beloved family and his amazing legacy.

To those who find joy in lifting others.
May you always know that the light you shine on others
is a brilliance of its own.

Introduction

"Mr. Red Carpet: From Harlem to Hollywood" is a great story about a great man who lived out his dream. That dream took him from Harlem, NY to Hollywood, CA. Not everyone is meant to stand in the spotlight, but those who support, uplift, and empower others are just as essential to success. This book tells the story of a man who worked behind the scenes for the biggest shows in Hollywood. He was a young boy with curiosity and a dream.

Whether you are a mentor, coach, strategist, or behind-the-scenes architect of success, your role is invaluable.

This book is not just about recognizing those roles—it's about celebrating them. It's about inspiring young readers to see the value in support, in service, and in the art of elevating others. Because when you choose to help others shine, you create a legacy of impact that extends far beyond yourself.

Let this book be a reminder: greatness isn't just about standing in the light. Sometimes, it's about being the reason the light shines at all.

Once upon a time, in a glittering city full of lights, tall buildings, and big dreams lived a young man named Anthony "Tony" Neely.

The city...... New York City. The Big Apple!

This is the beginning of the journey of a young man known as Mr. Red Carpet, who would become highlighted in this book.

Young Tony Neely was smart and curious. He always wanted to learn more about everything. In fact, Tony's mind was continuously curious about how things were made and how things worked.

Tony grew up in Harlem, a neighborhood in New York City's Upper Manhattan known for its rich culture and history. He lived with his mom and his older brother, Arnold. Mom Neely always made sure that Tony went to school every day.

Because of his academic success, Tony was accepted into the prestigious Aviation High School in New York. Tony was fascinated by how things were made, so discovering the mechanics of airplanes and what allowed them to soar high in the sky was really exciting.

After Tony graduated from Aviation High School, where he majored in flight engineering, he uncovered something else that sparked his interest. Tony fell in love with the theater. That's right. Tony loved the magic of storytelling coming to life on stage. He loved the lights and excitement of theater life.

Tony became a stagehand at local theaters to learn as much as he could about how to make a theater production come to life. His hard work paid off.

Guess what? Tony became stage manager for many Broadway plays. Broadway is home to New York City's biggest and most spectacular productions and musicals. Tony managed the behind-the-scenes operations involved in bringing theatrical productions to life. Tony worked with producers, set designers, and technical crews to ensure the productions were prepared, that they ran smoothly, and stayed within budget.

Tony worked on some of the biggest shows on Broadway including two Tony Award winning musicals. The Tony Award was formally known as the Antoinette Perry Award for Excellence in Broadway Theater. It is the most prestigious honor in American theater and it just happens to have the same name as Tony!

Tony toured across the United States with many productions. He met a lot of famous people in the entertainment industry including actors, producers, and skilled professionals such as lighting directors and art directors.

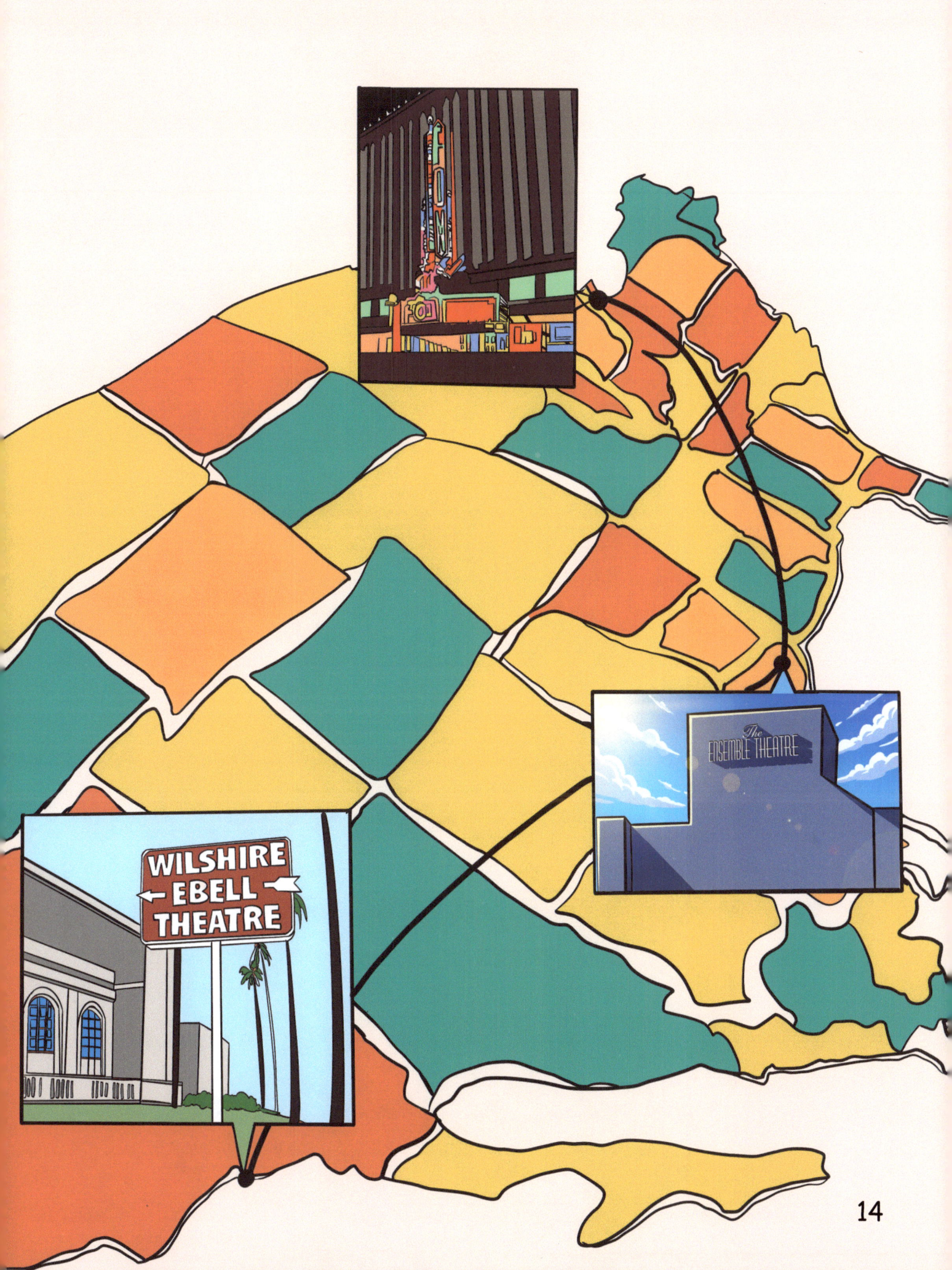

Tony was the life of every party, captivating everyone with his sensational stories from his experiences. He was a masterful storyteller.

Tony built a stellar reputation throughout New York, and his expertise soon caught the attention of another iconic city. Tony set his sights on Hollywood!!!

Hollywood is the epicenter for the film and television industry. Hollywood is famous for the home of television and movie studios. It has a rich history, and is an attraction for visitors around the world.

Tony made the big move from Harlem to Hollywood and became known as NY Tony. In fact, Tony had a personalized license plate that said NYTONY.

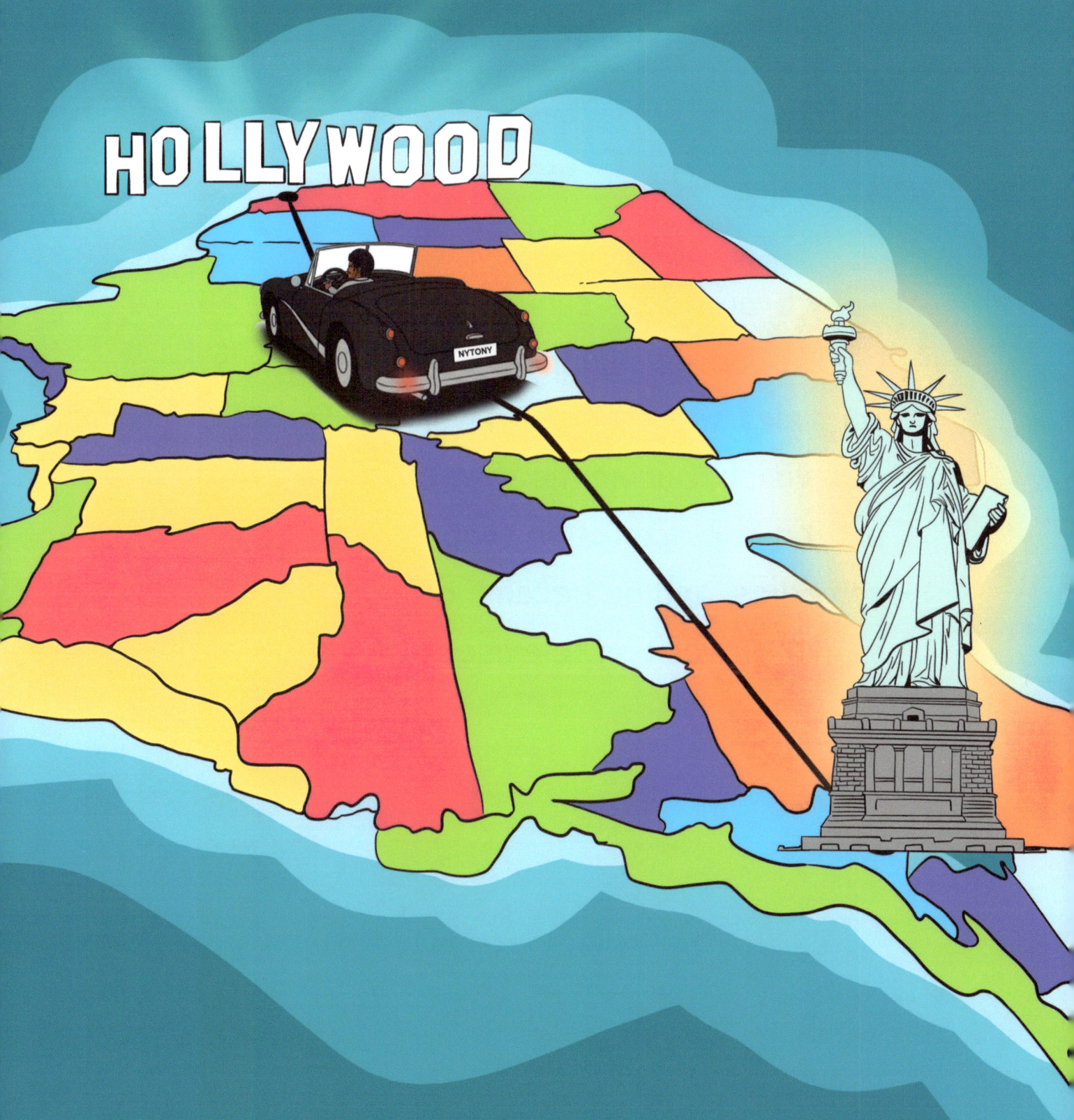

Tony brought his curiosity for making big productions happen. This time it was for television. He began working for ABC Television. During his time at ABC, he worked behind-the-scenes on soap operas and situation comedies, and he became a legend for his specialty work on televised award shows!

22

Tony is best known for his work on the Red Carpet! That's why this book is named "Mr. Red Carpet: From Harlem to Hollywood!" That's right! Tony was the man responsible for the Red Carpet at the arrivals of the legendary Academy Awards for twenty-two consecutive years.

The Academy Awards is also known as the Oscars and are widely considered to be the most prestigious awards in the film industry.

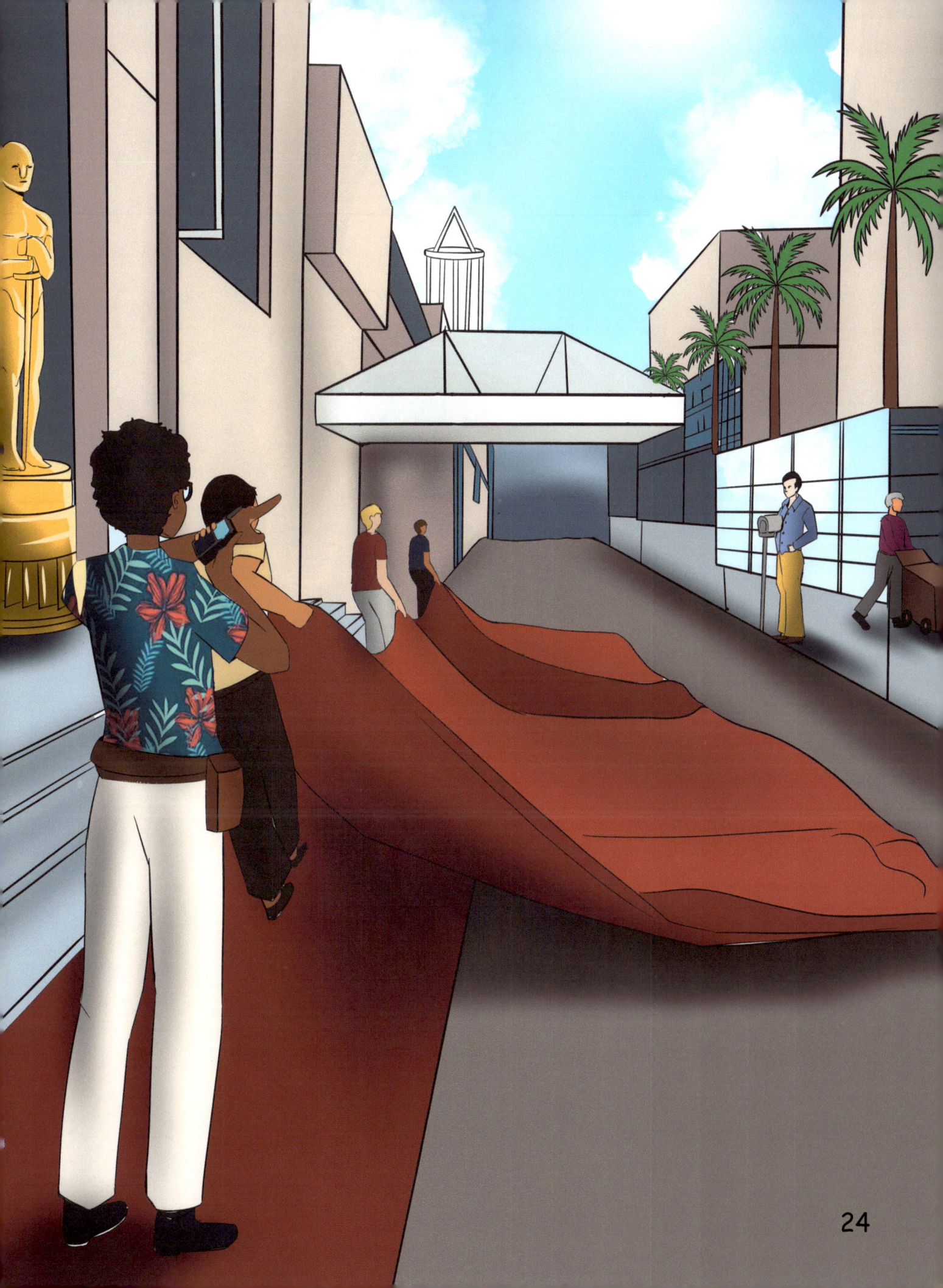

When the stars arrived for the most amazing night on television to celebrate film, Tony was there on the Red Carpet making things happen, and he made sure everything went perfectly on the most famous red carpet in the world.

Tony was responsible for the arrivals and press at the Oscars. He made sure that the Red Carpet was ready for the celebrities and the press who captured every moment. These moments were magnetic, electric, and magical. Tony knew that the Red Carpet was a place where dreams would come true for the actors and actresses who walked it. The arrivals at the coveted Oscars show would be broadcast to the world.

Because of Tony's knowledge of the needs of the arrivals and press areas for the Academy Awards, Tony was selected to help design the home of the Oscars, originally named the Kodak theater, now called the Dolby Theater on Hollywood Boulevard. It was an incredible honor for Tony. In fact, he walked the Red Carpet himself at the official groundbreaking for the Kodak Theater.

Tony handled the Red Carpet for other award shows including the Emmy Awards. The Emmy Awards is the premier recognition of artistic and technical merit for the television industry.

Tony's career, through his dedication and hard work, was magical and groundbreaking. What started as curiosity led to an incredible behind-the-scenes career in television and theater.

Tony never sought applause. He was a quiet superhero. The Red Carpet wasn't just for the stars—it was for him, too.

Tony Neely, Mr. Red Carpet, and NY Tony

"Mr. Red Carpet: From Harlem to Hollywood" is a true story highlighting the life of Anthony "Tony" Neely. He lived a commendable life that is acknowledged and appreciated. The following list is more of his career highlights, and a published article of his death published in the Hollywood Reporter and the Daily Variety, Hollywood's top news outlets at the time, and a poem remembering his life.

Career Highlights

Academy Awards, Production Manager for Arrivals and Press, for ABC for 22 years

Primetime Emmy Awards, ABC, CBS, NBC

Daytime Emmy Awards at Radio City Music Awards

American Film Institute (AFI) Awards

Production Manager 1984 Olympics

American Hero Awards

A Raisin in the Sun, Tony Award

Two Gentlemen of Verona, Tony Award

Bishop TD Jakes, Woman Thou Art Loosed

General Hospital, 227, Married With Children – TV Shows

James Brown at the Greek Theater

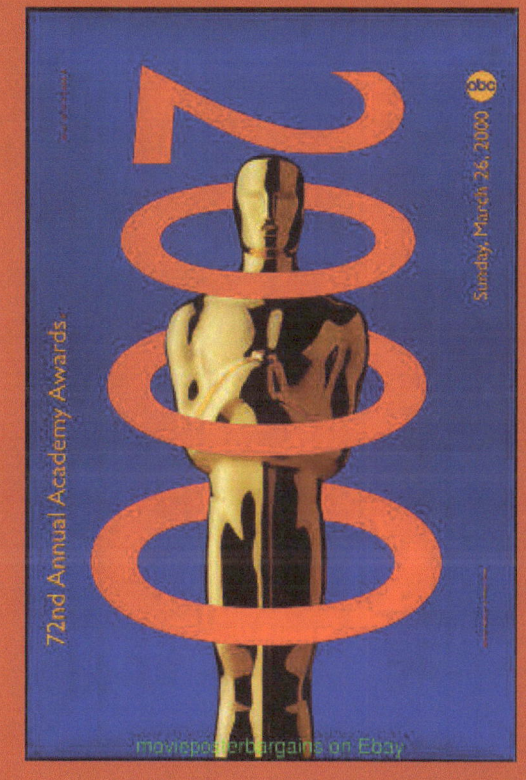

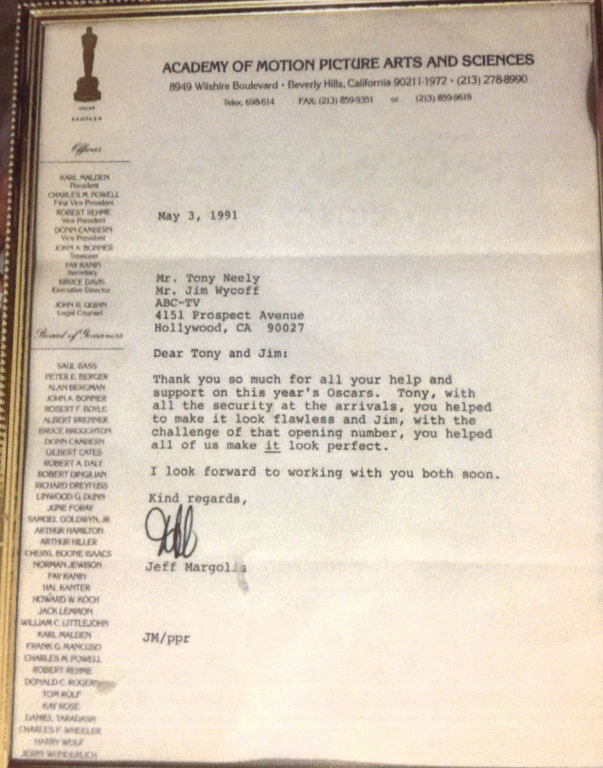

May 3, 1991

Mr. Tony Neely
Mr. Jim Wycoff
ABC-TV
4151 Prospect Avenue
Hollywood, CA 90027

Dear Tony and Jim:

Thank you so much for all your help and
support on this year's Oscars. Tony, with
all the security at the arrivals, you helped
to make it look flawless and Jim, with the
challenge of that opening number, you helped
all of us make it look perfect.

I look forward to working with you both soon.

Kind regards,

Jeff Margolis

JM/ppr

Associated Press News

By Empty, The Associated Press

June 11, 2009 12:57pm

Tony Neely, a stage manager and production manager in New York and Hollywood for more than three decades, died May 19 of liver cancer at his home in Castaic, Calif. He was 66.

Neely came to Disney/ABC in Hollywood in the late 1970's. He coordinated the press and arrival areas at the Academy Awards for 22 consecutive years and managed a wide range of production activities including sitcoms, game shows, soap operas, pilots, and events like the 1984 Summer Olympics. His credits also included the Daytime and Primetime Emmys and the NAACP Image Awards.

The Angel Award

Tony Neely
-Production Manager-
"Not in it for the money - But for the cause."

Hailing from New York City where he was Stage manager on two Tony Award Winning Musicals on Broadway. Tony Neely has graced the theatrical and television industry for nearly 23 years. As a Production Manager for ABC Television for 16 years, Tony has coordinated the Red Carpet Arrivals and Press areas for the highly televised *Academy Awards Show* for the last 18 years. Tony has managed the production activities of numerous sitcoms, game shows, and pilots. At a glance, his production credits include work on such shows as *General Hospital, The 1984 Olympic Games, 227, Married With Children,* and many more.

Now, as a freelance Production Manager and Consultant, Tony's production abilities been solicited for eight recent Emmy Awards shows, most recently being the *2000 Daytime and Primetime Emmy Awards.* Multi-talented, Tony's performed the role of Art Director for *James Brown* at the Greek

Theatre, and as Associate Producer with *Debbie Allen,* a Producer, Director, Dancer and Actress on a National Medical Awards show in Washington, D.C.

Tony has toured with the popular stage production, "Somebody Ought To Tell God Thank You," starring well-known Gospel singer Vickie Winans. He has also had the distinct pleasure of being production manager for Bishop T.D. Jakes Show, "Woman Thou Art Loosed."

Tony's exceptional experience and detailed knowledge of the production of the Academy Awards Landed him a role in the planning of the much anticipated "Hollywood & Highland" destination--the creation of a cornerstone for a Hollywood renaissance that will include a new live broadcast theatre to be the home of the Academy Awards beginning in March 2001.

Additionally, *Mr. Neely* has been the production manager for the *Multi-Cultural Prism Awards Gala* for five consecutive years.

Minorities in Business ♦ The 1998 Multi-Cultural Prism Awards Ceremony

Tony's access Badges

AMERICAN BROADCASTING COMPANIES, INC.

ANTHONY NEELY
NAME

PRODUCTION SERVICES
DEPARTMENT

62nd ANNUAL ACADEMY AWARDS

For Distinguished Achievement During 1989

©A.M.P.A.S.®

187

TONY NEELY

MARCH 26, 1990

Dorothy Chandler Pavilion

ANTHONY NEELY

PRODUCTION MANAGER

PRODUCTION

ALL ACCESS

2002 74th annual ACADEMY AWARDS®

SUNDAY, MARCH 24, 2002

4   4

55 emmy awards

Tony Neely

ACADEMY

EMMY 2003

Tony Neely - Mr. Red carpet

His past cannot be hidden.

It was already foretold.

The impact of those brought forward

Will never get old.

His life was not in vain.

His story has been told.

His footsteps echo through time.

His legacy carved in gold.

Through trials, he stood unshaken.

With wisdom, he lit the way.

His voice, now silent, still speaks,

Guiding our hearts to brighter days.

So, walk a path of honor.

Carry the torch he once bore.

For the Red Carpet was laid before you

To shine forevermore.

More inspiring and uplifting books by Blessons for Living can be found at www.blessonsforliving.com

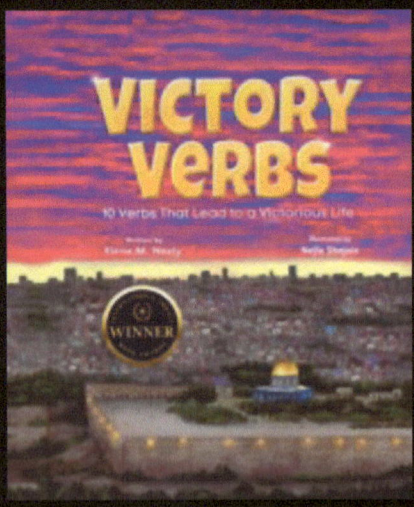

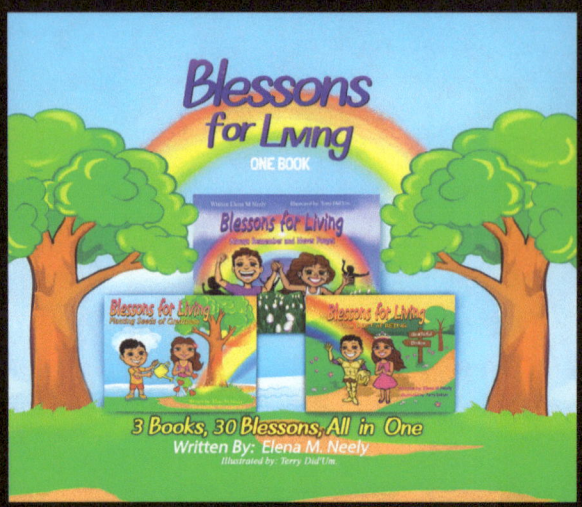

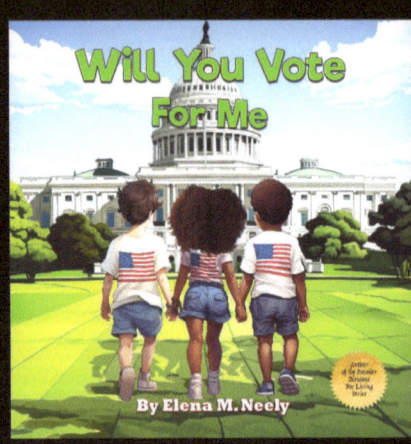

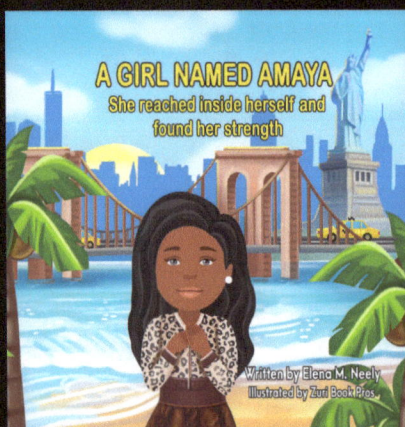

From the vibrant streets of Harlem to the dazzling lights of Hollywood, **Mr. Red Carpet: From Harlem to Hollywood** is the inspiring true story of Anthony "Tony" Neely—a man who built a legendary career making magic happen for the biggest names in entertainment. Born with an insatiable curiosity, young Tony Neely was fascinated by how things worked. Tony's journey took him from Broadway's grand stages to the heart of Hollywood's biggest productions. Though Tony never sought the spotlight, his story is one of perseverance, passion, and the power of those who work behind-the-scenes to bring dreams to life.

A celebration of curiosity, dedication, and the unsung heroes of entertainment, this book is a tribute to the man who made Hollywood's Red Carpet shine.

Elena M. Neely, MBA, Author/Publisher
Blessons For Living, LLC

Elena Neely is a thoughtful and intentional author, national speaker, and owner/publisher of Blessons for Living, LLC which is dedicated to aspiring youth and young adults to manifest a life of greatness. Blessons' purpose is to share life's greatest lessons with youth in an effort increase awareness, and to be a blessing to generations to come.
www.blessonsforliving.com